PRINTED IN THE UNITED STATES OF AMERICA

QUIET MIND
FOR KIDS

Braylee,
You are made for GREATNESS!
~ Collin Henderson

WRITTEN BY COLLIN HENDERSON & ALIKA ANTONE, PT, DPT
ILLUSTRATED BY ISABELLE MCANALLY

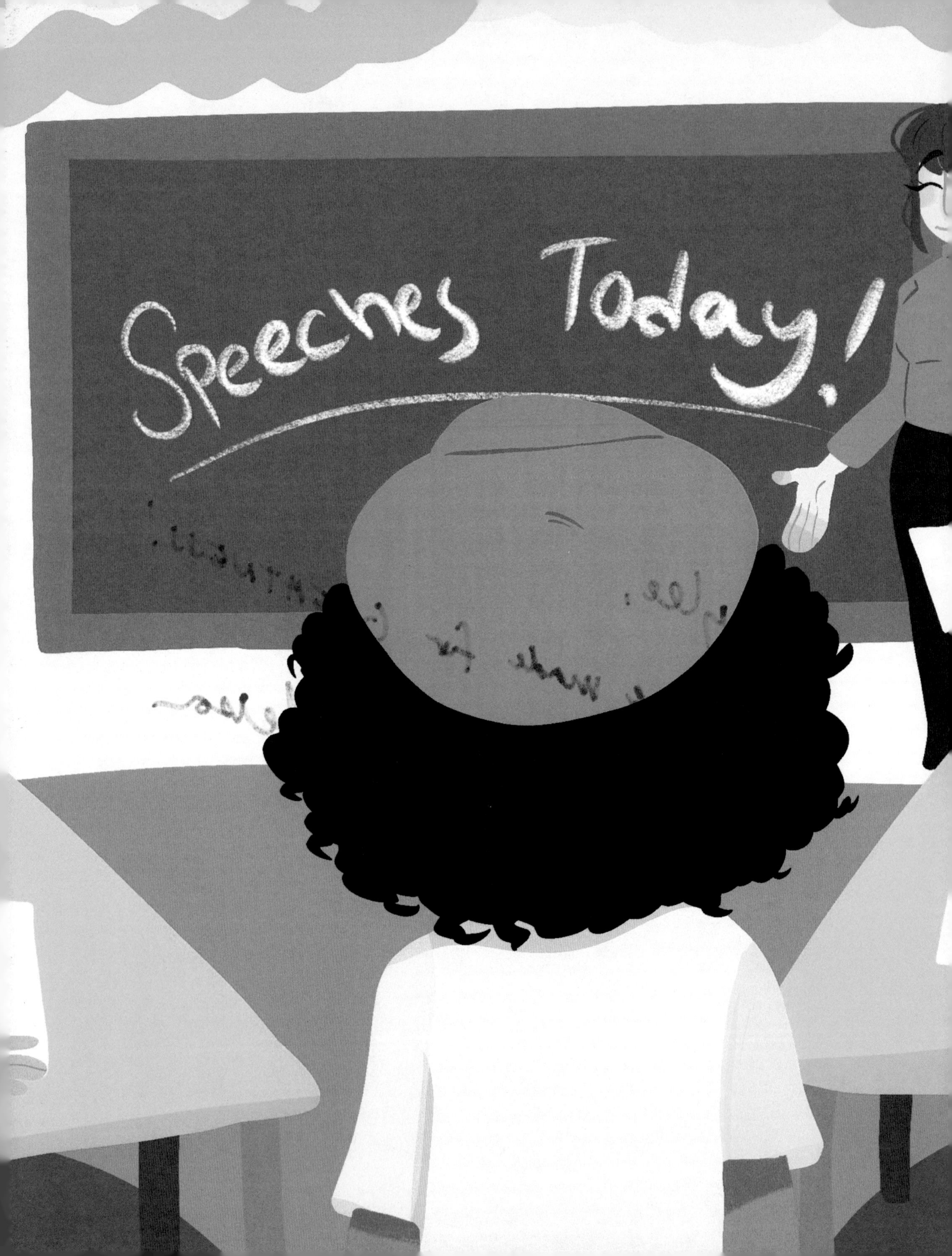
Speeches Today!

4 Steps...

Rey wanted to be her best:
Confident, brave, and kind.
She remembered the 4 steps
For how to quiet her mind.

Step one is to **BREATHE** slow, In the nose and out the lips. Just let the clean air flow. Like water passing ships.

Put one hand on your tummy,
Feel the air go in and out.
Remember to breathe in courage
And exhale out self-doubt.

Step two in this equation
Is to ENVISION your success.
Knowing what you want
Will help you lower stress.

You have everything you need already inside of YOU.
Close your eyes and imagine your goals coming true.

Now on to step three,
An important skill to train.
Positive SELF-TALK
Will supercharge your brain.

Saying nice things to yourself
Like: "I got this" and "I believe"
Will help program your mind
To see, dream, and achieve.

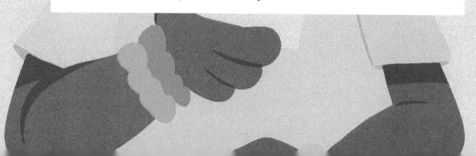

Step four is to be THANKFUL and think of what you have.
Happiness is a choice so train your brain to be glad.

When you focus on love,
Abundance, joy, and peace,
You'll improve your performance
And put your mind at ease.

With this mental system
Rey was able to be her BEST.
She gave a great speech
And aced her speaking test!

If you feel nervous or fear
and don't know what to do,
Train your mind like Rey.
This system will help you
through.

B is for BREATHE,
Take a few deep breaths.

E is for ENVISION,
Imagine your success.

S is for SELF-TALK,
To help improve your mood.

T is for THANKFUL,
Always focus on gratitude.

FLIP THE PAGE FOR MORE TIPS ON HOW TO TRAIN A QUIET MIND!

APPLICATION SECTION

Attention parents, teachers, and coaches! Help your children train a Quiet Mind by filling out this section. Encourage them to remember these words, thoughts, and emotions when they feel nerves, worry, or fear. Teach them to use the B.E.S.T. Method (Breathe. Envision. Self-Talk. Thankful.). All of these steps are backed by science to improve happiness, mood, and overall well-being.

Worry Check-In:
Help your child/student to identify situations or environments that cause them to feel worried, nervous, or afraid. Make a list here:

-
-
-

Help your child/student answer this question: Who is an adult that you trust that you can talk to about these feelings and emotions when they feel strong (family member, school counselor, coach, etc.)?

Let's build a Quiet Mind plan to work through these emotions.

BREATHE: Slow, deep breathing has been shown to lower stress and help the mind and body regain control. Have your child practice putting their hand on their tummy and breathe deep through their nose and out through their mouth. Physically show them how to do this. You should feel your diaphragm rise and fall with each inhale and exhale.

ENVISION: Write down three goals your child wants to accomplish or experience this year. Have them imagine and "visualize" these goals daily to help create a clear picture for their brain. The key is to train your mind to focus on what you want, not what you don't want. Have them think of this list when they need motivation. Help them identify and write down these goals below.

School Goal:

Life Goal:

Hobby or Extra-Curricular Activity Goal:

What are three actions or habits you commit to do to help you reach these goals?

1.

2.

3.

SELF-TALK: Help your child write down three "affirmations," which is another word for positive self-talk. Start with the phrase "I am." Have them memorize these phrases and say them daily and when they need a confidence boost (For example: I am brave. I am a hard worker. I am strong.). Remove the words "can't" and "don't" from your vocabulary, and focus on productive language. Words create pictures in our brain that influence feelings and actions. This type of positive self-talk has been proven to be one of the best strategies to improve confidence and performance.

Reminder for parents, teachers, and coaches: Let the child pick their own words that mean something to them, not your words.

I am:

I am:

I am:

THANKFUL: It's hard to feel fear, doubt, anger, and GRATITUDE at the same time. Thus, help your child train their brain to focus on what they have, not on what they don't have. Gratitude and optimism have been shown to lower stress and blood pressure, boost your immune system, and improve resilience. Adopting a gratitude routine as a family is a fantastic way to help train a Quiet Mind. You can do this during meals, school drop-off, and before sports, music, dance, or other performance settings. Help your child identify and list what they are most grateful for in four categories. Have them think of this list when they need a happiness boost.

People:

Places:

Things:

Experiences:

Great job! Remind your child to review these powerful reminders daily. It's important not to simply read or think about them, but rather to FEEL them as well. Make this a daily mindset practice just like exercising and eating healthy foods. Your child's brain needs to be trained too! Finding your breath, visualizing success, using productive self-talk, and practicing gratitude are powerful mental muscles to strengthen, that have the direct power to set a chain reaction for more positive things to follow.

MENTAL CONDITIONING MINDFULNESS SCRIPT

What we think, say, see, hear, and experience all play a role in the conditioning of our mind – especially in our youth. How you speak to your child becomes their self-talk and identity. With this in mind, parents, coaches, and teachers – read this mindfulness script to help your child program a Quiet Mind.

Using the B.E.S.T. Method, we will guide you through the steps to improve your child's self-awareness, confidence, and overall well-being. If we can teach them these mental skills now, the sky's the limit! Let's not wait for a problem, but instead be PROACTIVE with their mindset and mental fitness.

Quiet Mind Script (parents, coaches, and teachers, read this out loud to your kids)

BREATHE
Sitting or lying in a comfortable position, quiet your mind and body by taking a slow deep breath. With your eyes closed, gently breathe in through your nose and out through your mouth. Put your hand on your tummy and feel it get big as you breathe in, and smaller as you breathe out. Don't rush, but slowly breathe in through your nose and out through your mouth.

Whenever you feel scared, worried, or nervous, remember to find your breath and breathe. Continue to keep your eyes closed and take three more slow deep breaths.

[Pause]

ENVISION
Now, daydream and imagine something you want. What is your goal? What do you want to experience or achieve? Think back to the goals you wrote down in this book. Thoughts become things.

Imagine yourself being happy and achieving those goals now.

See yourself having a great day at school or with your siblings and friends. Imagine what that would look like.
[Pause]

Now think of something you want to accomplish outside of school (help them identify this in an area they are passionate about... could be a club, sport, music, dance, or extra-curricular activity)

Imagine you are actually doing that activity and achieving that goal now. What are you seeing? What are you feeling? What are you wearing? Who is around you? Pretend you are there in your mind experiencing those things now.

[Pause]

SELF-TALK
With your eyes still shut, practice saying nice things to yourself. Think of the affirmations you wrote down in this book. Say those to yourself now in your mind.

(Adults, feel free to remind them of their "I am" statements)

[Pause]

It's hard to be good at something with negative self-talk. That is why we have to train our brain to be positive. Let's practice positive self-talk now.

Think of times when you did something that made you proud or happy. Relive and think of those experiences now.

[Pause]

Now think of times when someone said something nice about you and gave you a compliment. What kind things do people say about you? Think about those things.

[Pause]

Now think of all of the hard work you have been doing to achieve your goal. With your eyes still shut, remember all the things you have been doing to practice, study, and prepare to be your best and achieve your dreams.

[Pause]
THANKFUL
It's important to always remember what you are thankful for. It's often easy to think about what you don't have. This will not help you be your best. Train your mind to think about what you do have. Gratitude is a super power for your brain.

Take a moment to think and feel gratitude in these areas...

First, think about people you are grateful for, who love you, and make you happy.

[Pause]

Now, think of places you like to go that make you feel joy.

[Pause]

Finally, think of things you play with or things you do and experience that make you happy.

[Pause]

Whenever you feel worried or nervous, think of these things to help quiet your mind and be brave.

As we conclude this mindfulness session, it's important to always remember who you are. With your eyes still shut, say these truths out loud:

I am kind...

I am loved...

I am brave...

I am worthy.

Great job! With your eyes open now, never forget, whatever the brain can see, and believe, it can achieve. You can be anything you put your mind to. I care about you, and believe in you; and want you to remember this one simple truth: The body has limits, but the mind is limitless. You are limitless.

Quiet Mind for Kids is written by acclaimed mental performance coach and father of five children, Collin Henderson, and co-authored by one of the most respected physical therapist in the Pacific Northwest (and father of four kids), Dr. Alika Antone. The amazing illustrations in the book were created by the talented Isabelle McAnally. Quiet Mind for Kinds was edited by Sarah Johnson and Kate Bethell.

To reach Collin Henderson, visit thecollinhenderson.com or find him on social media @collinhenderson. Collin and his family live in Nashville, Tennessee.

To connect with Dr. Alika Antone, visit www.a2pt.family or follow @qm4kids on Instagram. Alika and his family live in Tacoma, Washington.

Made in the USA
Middletown, DE
11 September 2021